LIFE
in the
BLOOD

Apostle Juanita L. Ford

Kingdom Builders Publications LLC

Life in the Blood
Copyright © 2002 by Juanita Ford
2016 Kingdom Builders Publications

All rights reserved. No part of this book may be reproduced or transmitted in any form or by any means without written permission from the author.

Paperback ISBN: 9780692756645
Cover Designer – LoMar Designs

Editors:
Kingdom Builders Publications
Vision Works,
P. O. Box 373439
Decatur, GA 30037

Reprint 2016 in USA
Go to this website for bookings and ordering:
www.kingdombuilderspublications.com

All Holy Scriptures are taken from the King James Version of the Bible unless otherwise stated.
Scripture quotations marked (AMP) are taken from The Amplified Bible, Old Testament copyright Ó 1965, 1987 by the Zondervan Corporation. The Amplified Bible New Testament copyright
©1958, 1987 by the Lockman Foundation. Used by permission.

TABLE OF CONTENTS

	Acknowledgments	4
	Preface	5
1	The Miracle in New Beginnings	7
2	Recognizing the Devil's Attack	13
3	The Source of Life	22
4	Transformed by the Blood	27
5	Fighting the Good Fight	35
6	A New Way of Life	41
	About the Author	47

ACKNOWLEDGMENTS

I thank my Heavenly Father for allowing me to share my testimony through the writing of this book. His saving grace still amazes me! I also thank my husband, Apostle Charles Ford, for encouraging and assisting me in every way throughout this project.

Thanks to:

My late parents, J.C. & Mary Lovett

My brother, J.C. Lovett, Jr.

My sisters, Gloria Jean Bell & Margaret Ann Lovett

My nieces, Kim & Katina Bowers

My beloved church family at Full Benefit Ministries Development Center

My spiritual parents, Apostles Henry & Ann Jones

Dr. Creflo & Taffi Dollar and World Changers Ministry

Pastor Denise and (the late) Lee Armstrong and the Beauty for Ashes World Outreach Ministry

Evangelist Ann Randolph

I especially thank Kingdom Builders Publications for publishing my book, Victory Through the Blood and who made this project possible, again. I also thank my writer/editor, Yolanda Brown (VisionWorks) for making this book enjoyable and easy to understand. Thank you both for supporting me in every area of book development. Much love!

Finally, I thank everyone who rendered prayers, support and encouragement during this journey. God bless each of you!

PREFACE

If someone you knew and trusted told you of an over-the-counter medicine that could cure whatever ails you, would you try it? What if every member of that person's family had taken it and experienced 100% recovery, would you be willing to give it a try? I certainly would.

It may sound hard to believe, but this medicine actually exists. It's not some New Age drug, neither is it an illegal substance. It is the awesome, wonder-working power of the Blood of Jesus! When taken as directed, the blood produces miraculous results. Once you try it, your life will never be the same again. I've tried it and it can't be beaten!

I discovered the power of the blood a few years ago when I was diagnosed with fibroid tumors. At the time, I was laying on a hospital bed with an irregular heartbeat and a temperature of 107. If you know anything about the typical outcome of people who suffer fevers of this magnitude, you know that there was little likelihood that I'd ever live to write this book. Today I am totally healed!

God's mercy and ever-enduring love for us never ceases to amaze me. The Bible tells us that everything is the Lord's. And yet, He has given us access to everything He owns for our enjoyment *(1 Timothy 6:17)*. Not only that, He has given us the power to rule

and reign in life. That means we can also rule over our circumstances.

You may be experiencing challenges in your life right now. If you are, there is a way out. On the other hand, everything in your life may be going quite well. That's good news. You too can benefit. After reading this book, you will begin walking in a new freedom that can only be found in the dynamic life force of the Blood of Jesus.

You will begin to see change in what you thought were impossible situations and you will be equipped to conquer every challenge that may arise in the future. You will know, once and for all, that there is Life in the Blood!

THE MIRACLE IN NEW BEGINNINGS
Chapter One

We are each faced with challenges in life that we are expected to somehow overcome. The reality, however, is that many of us fall into situations with no idea of how we will get out of them and little hope that we ever will. Right now you may be in a situation for which you have no solution. In fact, you may have tried a number of things to remedy the problem with little or no success. You could be experiencing challenges in your health, finances, marriage or other challenging issues.

In *John 10:10,* the Word of God reveals that Jesus came to give us "life and life more abundantly." When we are living in lack, confusion, depression and poor health, we are not experiencing the abundant life that God has predestined for us. We are living as if we do not have the privilege of His promise.

When you experience challenges in your life, realize that the way you choose to handle these experiences will determine your outcome. If you go through challenges feeling defeated and distressed, you will be defeated and distressed. On the other hand, if you go through them with the faith and confidence that you will overcome them, you will!

Many people believe that once they become saved,

they are immune to difficult circumstances. That couldn't be further from the truth. In fact, Jesus tells us in the Amplified Version of *John 16:33*, "...In the world [we will] have tribulation and trials and distress and frustration...." He also warns us not to allow life's challenges to get the best of us because He has already conquered every battle for us!

Whatever battle you go through, realize that God already has the winning solution. All you need to do is consult Him for guidance and remain confident that His plan is best. His plan will always promote your well-being.

God's Original Plan

When God created man, His plans for our lives were far different from what we are experiencing today. His original intent was for us to rule the earth. In fact, He created us to be like Him: to look, act and live like Him.

Think about it. Have you ever read a scripture that suggested that God needed anything? Do you recall any verse that describes how He overcame sickness or paid His rent? Better yet, have you ever read where He needed clothes, food or supplies of any kind?

Adam and Eve had no need to buy groceries or visit the doctor. Everything they needed was right there in the garden. God blessed them with a beautiful home, excellent health and the freedom to choose what they wanted when they wanted it. Not only that, He told them to be fruitful, multiply, replenish the earth and subdue it (*Genesis 1:28*).

According to the Amplified Bible, the word subdue

means "to use all of the earth's resources to serve God and man." In essence, God was saying, "Hey guys, help yourselves to everything I own. It's yours, enjoy it!" As long as Adam and Eve remained in God's will, they were able to enjoy the freedom and comfort of the "good life."

Likewise, God intends for us to live the "good life." He never intended for us to endure sickness and disease, poverty or unhappiness. He desired then, just as He desires today, that we enjoy the benefits of a prosperous and healthy life. "Beloved, I pray that you may prosper in every way and [that your body] may keep well, even as [I know] your soul keeps well" (*3 John 2, AMP*).

In *Genesis 5:5* we learn that Adam lived nine hundred and thirty years. That's a long time. These days, it is very rare that we ever hear of people living beyond seventy or eighty years old. The maximum is generally just above one hundred years. Generally we consider that age a miracle!

I am convinced that God intended for each of us to live without experiencing death. His plans never changed; man changed. When Adam and Eve made the unfortunate decision to eat from the Tree of Good and Evil, God had to enforce plan "B".

Plan "B"

Under this new plan, God created a way for us to regain the power and freedom He initially established for us. Because He sent His Son, Jesus, to die for our sin, we are able to enjoy the benefits that God originally intended for us to have.

When Jesus shed His blood for us, it served as atonement for our sins. To atone means "to completely wipe away." In other words, reconciliation between God and man was achieved through the life, death and resurrection of Jesus Christ. His blood doesn't cover our sin, it destroys it!

Jesus died so that the will of His Father would be fulfilled in our lives. His death had nothing to do with His relationship to the Father. His pain and suffering was for our sake and our sake alone. God loves us just that much!

In *Luke 4:18*, Jesus announces His Heavenly assignment; "The Spirit of the Lord is upon me, because he hath anointed me to preach the gospel to the poor; he hath sent me to heal the brokenhearted, to preach deliverance to the captives, and recovering of sight to the blind, to set at liberty them that are bruised."

The Amplified Bible records in verse 19 that Jesus came "To proclaim the accepted and acceptable year of the Lord [the day when salvation and the free favors of God profusely abound]." I like the words "profusely abound." Profusely means "to give freely, abundantly and extravagantly." To abound means "to be great in number or amount." In other words, God wants to shower us with abundant and extravagantly huge amounts of favor. Hallelujah!

The purpose of the Blood of Jesus is to mend or replace whatever is missing or broken in our lives. God anointed (empowered) Jesus with the ability to correct our misfortunes and make whatever is wrong right.

Newness of Life

As a result of the shed blood of Jesus, we have a blood-bought right to come before God with our concerns. We have the privilege of standing before Him without shame, guilt or condemnation. There is nothing that we can do to earn His love or forgiveness. Jesus took care of all of that when He died on the cross.

When we accept Jesus as our Lord and Savior, we give up our way of doing things to pursue God's plans. The Bible says, "If [you] confess with [your] mouth the Lord Jesus, and shall believe in [your] heart that God hath raised him from the dead, [you] shall be saved. For with the heart man believeth unto righteousness; and with the mouth confession is made unto salvation" (*Romans 10: 9,10*). When you begin living according to His purpose, you enter the born-again experience.

The simple acceptance of Jesus through your belief makes you righteous. To be righteous means "you are in right standing with God." It does not mean that you are perfect. He knew that we could not be perfect, so He created a way for us to make things right with Him when we mess up. It's called repentance. Repentance is not an apology. It is a decision to turn away from the direction you are going to the direction God would have you to go.

Righteousness is a free gift that God gives to those who accept His Son. There is nothing you can do to earn it. Good deeds can't earn your right standing with God. Being a good person, giving to the poor or joining a church can't make you righteous either. Your belief and acceptance of what Jesus has already done establishes your righteousness. Righteousness serves as your coat of protection and assurance.

The night before He died, Jesus had communion with the disciples. Communion represents the body and blood of our Lord and Savior, Jesus Christ. When we partake of His communion, we recall what He did for us. As He gave the bread to the disciples, Jesus said, "…This is my body which is given for you; this do in remembrance of me" (*Luke 22:19*). Then in verse 20, He took the cup and said, "…This cup is the new testament in my blood, which is shed for you."

Because of His blood, you can start fresh today. His blood not only makes it possible to erase your past mistakes, it makes possible new beginnings. This very day you can begin living a new and better life. There are no conditions to meet, except that you know and accept Jesus. That's it. It's not like qualifying for a house or establishing credit. Jesus already paid the price when He died on the cross. No matter what you've done or how much you've been through, new life can begin today.

Give God the opportunity to begin a new work in you. He has plans for your life that were established before the beginning of time. The Amplified Version of *Ephesians 2:10* reads, "For we are God's own handiwork (His workmanship), recreated in Christ Jesus, [born anew] that we may do those good works which God predestined (planned beforehand) for us [taking paths which He prepared ahead of time], that we should walk in them [living the good life which He prearranged and made ready for us to live]."

My friend, there is nothing too hard for God. He is the same yesterday, today and forever. He never changes and that's good news!

RECOGNIZING THE DEVIL'S ATTACK
Chapter Two

When I first began experiencing the physical ailments that led to fibroid tumors, I did not immediately recognize what was going on. I would often feel tired and experience pain in my lower abdomen. My feet began to swell and I had no tolerance for certain foods, particularly dairy products and meat. I had been experiencing these painful effects for nearly 2 years before I actually went to the doctor.

In 1996, God began to guide me in a study on the Blood of Jesus. There was no connection in my mind between the health challenges I was experiencing and this study. In obedience to God, I began studying the subject. I looked up scriptural references concerning "the blood" in the concordance. A friend of mine also let me borrow a set of tapes concerning the power found in the Blood of Jesus.

I listened to the series of teachings for months. One particular point that stood out in the teaching centered on the absence of songs and teachings about the blood in today's church. The minister suggested that when such references to the Blood of Jesus are absent, the life of the church (God's people) suffers and can ultimately cease to exist.

You see, the natural body depends on blood to supply life. Likewise, the Blood of Jesus adds life to the Body of Christ. Whether we're singing songs about it, reading about it or teaching it, it adds vitality to those who hear it.

The Blood of Jesus also renders Satan helpless in his attack against the church. He wants to bring in things like deceit, adultery, fornication and jealousy. These acts of the flesh wound the Body of Christ and the human body as well. Sin cripples its victims physically, spiritually and emotionally.

Life in the Blood

Many of the scriptures I read during my study shed new light on the subject. This one, however, made a lasting impression in my spirit. "For the life of the flesh is in the blood: and I have given it to you upon the altar to make an atonement for your souls: for it is the blood that maketh an atonement for the soul" (*Leviticus 17:11*).

"The life of the flesh is in the blood." Isn't that awesome? That was new revelation to me. The fact that the very life force of my body is found in the Blood of Jesus propelled me to begin a whole new way of thinking. If you're like me, you probably think that the life force for your body is your heart. After all, it is the muscle used to pump blood into other parts of the body. Blood rids us of bacteria, germs, infection and disease. Without it, the body cannot function. It will collapse and die.

The same is true for those who exist without the Blood of Jesus. Eventually, they will collapse and die. Without Jesus, they are spiritually dead. Ultimately, they will experience physical death and exist no more. Without the Blood of Jesus, no one can live eternally with the Father. Neither can they experience the healing benefits of its power on earth.

The Blood of Jesus is vital to our total existence. Through His blood, we are recreated and made whole again. Not just in the spiritual sense, but in the physical and emotional aspects of our lives as well. Although the heart is necessary for our physical existence, the Blood of Jesus is the spiritual life source by which the Body of Christ functions.

In some Bibles, *Leviticus 17:11* leads the reader to *Romans 3:24-26*. This is the *Amplified Version* of that scripture in Romans:

[All] are justified and made upright and in right standing with God, freely and gratuitously by His grace (His unmerited favor and mercy), through the redemption which is [provided] in Christ Jesus, Whom God put forward [before the eyes of all] as a mercy seat and propitiation by His blood [the cleansing and life-giving sacrifice of atonement and reconciliation, to be received] through faith. This was to show God's righteousness, because in His divine forbearance He had passed over and ignored former sins without punishment. It was to demonstrate and prove at the present time (in the now season) that He Himself is righteous and that He justifies and accepts as righteous him who has [true] faith in Jesus.

There's a lot of meat in this scriptural reference. It further defines the Blood of Jesus as a "cleansing and life-giving sacrifice of atonement and reconciliation." Paul also advises us to *receive* the blood by faith.

You may say, "The reason I'm suffering now is because of something I did in the past." Look at the next line of the preceding scripture. In essence, it says that because of God's goodness and mercy toward us, He has chosen to pass over and ignore our former sins without punishment. So if you're thinking that the things you're enduring are punishment from God, think again. They may be a result of the choices you made or consequences for those choices, but they are not some form of punishment by God.

God desires only good for us. He never wants anything other than what is best for us. Why else would He go through the trouble of sacrificing His Son and enforcing a back-up plan to restore us to right standing with Him? It's simple, He loves us!

Easier than We Think

I am sure that when we all get to Heaven, we'll be disappointed to find out how easy God made it for us. Actually, I'm beginning to realize it now. He's given us His Word, the Bible, to guide us in everything we do. It contains His thoughts, plans and direction for our lives. In it, there are warnings and consequences for doing things our way, and there are rewards for doing them His way. The Bible is filled with promises, many that we do not know or believe.

In our human nature, it is sometimes difficult to believe that God wants to be as good to us as He says. We have been told that we are nothing; filthy rags unworthy of His goodness. That is so untrue. He has given us everything that pertains to life and godliness (*2 Peter 1:3*). He has also given us Jesus.

When we pray according to God's will and call on the name of Jesus, He immediately begins to intercede on our behalf. In other words, He goes before His Father's throne to present and settle the matter. His purpose is to remove the burdens in our lives (*Isaiah 10:27*). Burdens can be identified as sickness and disease, problematic relationships, lack, confusion, depression or grief. Anything or anyone that weighs you down or keeps you out of the will of God is a burden.

God never intended for us to worry or "stress out" about the things that concern us. Jesus says very clearly in *Matthew 6:25-34* that we should not worry. Instead, He encourages us to seek first the kingdom of God. That means we should seek God's way of doing things rather than relying on our own abilities.

Just as any good father would do, God wants to take care of us. In verse 32, Jesus expresses that our Heavenly Father already knows our needs. He simply wants us to ask Him for what we need. Asking opens the door. By asking, we surrender our concerns. That means we no longer worry about them because we are certain that God can and will handle them. Asking also establishes that God is our Source.

We are so conditioned to doing things on our own. It is the way we were taught, but it's not the Master's plan. God is concerned about everything that concerns us, no matter how small or insignificant it may seem. David says it with such confidence in *Psalm 138:8*, "The Lord will perfect that which concerneth me…." He didn't say, "Maybe the Lord will perfect that which concerneth me." He said, "God will!"

Whether it's having enough food to eat, clothes to wear or a car to drive, if it's important to you, it's important to God. Remember you have a blood-bought right to go before Him without guilt or condemnation. When you pray, expect God to hear, answer and intervene. Leave it alone. Don't concern yourself with how or when He will handle it. Move out of the way and rest in His promises.

The Weapons of Warfare

A man or woman who recognizes God's purpose for his or her life cannot be stopped! The sooner you begin to realize your purpose, the sooner you'll recognize that the devil's mission is to defeat you. God has given you supernatural abilities to overcome the challenges in your life. However, you must know what they are and begin to activate them.

One weapon is obedience. *Deuteronomy 28:1-14* clearly describes the blessings the Lord has for those who obey His commandments and live according to His statutes. I love reading these verses because they outline the inheritance package God wants us to enjoy here on earth. He promises to bless us in all that we do. He also promises to prosper us in houses, land, wealth and children.

When we obey God, we avoid the pitfalls of disobedience. Pitfalls are the consequences we experience as a result of our failure to do things His way. God can and will speak to you through His Word. He will also speak to you through dreams, visions and confirmation.

Although I did not know it at the time, my decision to obey God by studying the purpose and power of Jesus' blood led to my healing. It also led me into a new path of ministry. As a result of my obedience, thousands will be blessed!

Another weapon against the devil's attack is prayer. Prayer is simply talking to God and listening to His response. So often we blurt out all of our concerns to Him without expecting that He will answer right away. I don't know, maybe we think He needs to roll our concerns over in His head a time or two before coming up with a solution. No! God has the solution even before we ask. "Ask, and it shall be given you; seek, and ye shall find; knock, and it shall be opened unto you…" (*Matthew 7:7*).

"And this is the confidence we have in him, that, if we ask any thing according to his will, he heareth us; And if we know he hear us, whatsoever we ask, we know that we have the petitions that we desired of him" (*1 John 5: 14-15*). You can't find a better deal than that!

When we repeat God's Word back to Him during prayer, He has no alternative except to answer. His Word is His promise and it will always accomplish the purpose for which He sent it (*Isaiah 55:11*). Always remember to include God's Word in your prayers. Repeat back to Him what He has already said. You'll always get an answer.

Praise is a third weapon. The devil can't stand it! It just blows his mind when we praise God before our situations are resolved. This is the best time to praise God. In *2 Chronicles 20:21,22* we see the enemies of

Jehoshaphat and his people destroyed right before their very eyes. Although they were outnumbered and their defeat was inevitable, the Word of the Lord came to them saying, "…the battle is not yours, but God's" (verse 15). "Ye shall not need to fight in this battle…fear not, nor be dismayed…for the Lord will be with you" (verse 17).

When Jehoshaphat realized that God was with him, it increased his confidence and he and the people began to worship God. The day they were expected to enter into battle, Jehoshaphat rose early and appointed singers to go ahead of the army. When they began to sing and praise, their enemies began to fight amongst each other and they defeated themselves. When they were all dead, Jehoshaphat and his people went to the enemy's camp and recovered precious jewels, clothing and goods. There was so much that it took three days to gather it all!

Praise is a powerful weapon against the enemy. It not only confuses the devil, it stills him completely!

THE SOURCE OF LIFE
Chapter Three

During my illness, I began to realize that the fibroid tumors on my uterus were not only a physical attack, but a spiritual attack as well. The Holy Spirit began to reveal more about the connection between the two to my husband Charles and I.

As we continued to seek God, we began to better understand the purpose for the devil's attack. You see, those tumors had begun to suck the life out of my body. Other parts of my body were beginning to malfunction. I realized that the place where the tumors existed was the very same place that God specifically designed to bring new life into this world. The womb!

Over the years, I'd heard numerous women complain about fibroid tumors. It became clear to me that not only was I being attacked, but women all over the world were being attacked! The devil is constantly after our seed (children). He's been working the same plan since he tempted Eve in the garden.

An Ongoing Battle

In *Genesis 3:15*, God placed a spirit of animosity between the woman and the serpent. "And I will put enmity between thee and the woman, and between thy seed and her seed...." In that same verse God warns that the woman's seed would bruise the serpent's head.

We see the reality of this warning through the life, death and resurrection of Jesus Christ. *Galatians 4:4-7* says:

"But when the fullness of the time was come, God sent forth his Son, made of a woman, made under the law, To redeem them that were under the law, that we might receive the adoption of sons. And because ye are sons, God hath sent forth the Spirit of his Son into your hearts, crying, Abba, Father, Wherefore thou art no more a servant, but a son, and if a son, then an heir of God through Christ."

In other words, Jesus came to restore our right standing with God. He provided the opportunity for us to return to our rightful positions as sons and daughters of the Most High.

Notice however, that Jesus entered through the same gate that we entered...the womb of a woman. God uses the womb to bring new life into this world. The devil wants to foil that plan. He wants to defeat God's plans by depleting woman's ability to produce children!

Through childbirth, God has given women the awesome opportunity to co-create with Him. When a child is conceived, it is nurtured and developed inside the protective walls of its mother's stomach. Her entire body changes through this dynamic metamorphosis.

God fully equips women for childbearing. Just as the body flexes automatically to carry the child, it also flexes to produce food after birth. It is such a miraculous privilege. Think about it: the baby cries and the woman's breasts immediately drip milk. She doesn't have to struggle to produce it. It's already there. Even when a mother is away from her child, her body informs her that the baby is hungry.

Our Heavenly Father is no different. Whatever we need, He provides. All we need do is ask. It's that simple.

Women are highly favored by God. We learn this in the book of Luke when the angel appeared to Mary declaring her empowerment and favor. Why? Because Mary was chosen as the vessel by which "new life" would begin for each of us through Jesus.

Now you can better understand why the devil is so desperate to end the birth cycle. I think he strategically picks who he wants as his next victim. Women who are faithful to God and likely to produce godly offspring are, I believe, his primary target.

For this reason, women must always be on guard. Understand, I am not saying that women should live fearfully, but they should be able to recognize when the devil is launching an attack against them. Later in the book, I will share with you things you can do in the natural and spiritual realms to render the devil's attack ineffective.

A Joint Effort

Women have a special role in God's creation. This statement does not serve to discredit men. They too are valuable in that they produce the seed and serve as the head and provider of the home. A woman's womb, however, is the avenue by which life is ushered into the world. There is no other way. Although each of us has been given an important task to accomplish, the primary assignment given to women is to reproduce.

In *Ephesians 5:23*, women are likened to the church. It is an interesting comparison and one that I believe warrants further explanation. While women are designed to bring forth new life in the earth, the church is also designed to foster new life by leading others to Christ.

In a previous chapter, I mentioned that our acceptance of Jesus Christ precedes the born-again experience. When we begin living according to God's plan, we make a conscious decision to play by His rules. By that I mean we actively practice His precepts. We act appropriately and obey His commandments. When we fail, we repent and continue the journey.

Have you ever noticed the number of women who attend church? Women visited Jesus' tomb and later announced His resurrection. They were the carriers of the message. Today women are the corner stone of our churches. They intercede on behalf of the pastor, the church and the ministry overall. They also give birth to great men and women of God: apostles, prophets, evangelists, pastors and teachers. These are the five-fold ministry gifts given to the Body of Christ, by God, to carry out His work (*Ephesians 4:11-13*).

Women are gifts of great value and should be respected as such. They are co-creators with God in the fulfillment of His master plan. For example, God gave Eve to Adam as a gift because she was the only suitable partner for him. She added balance to his existence and assisted him in carrying out his God-given assignment.

TRANSFORMED BY THE BLOOD
Chapter Four

When a woman is diagnosed with fibroid tumors, she risks the chance of infertility. Such tumors hinder and often times bring closure to the birth cycle. Tumors also draw blood from other parts of the body, making it difficult for the body to function properly. As a matter of fact, they can become enlarged during the monthly flow.

Let's educate ourselves briefly about fibroid tumors from a medical perspective.

A fibroid is a non-cancerous tumor that arises from the uterine muscle and connecting tissue. Since they develop following the onset of menstruation, enlarge during pregnancy and decrease in size after menopause, fibroids are thought to be estrogen dependent.

One in five women in the United States has at least some evidence of fibroids, with most occurring in women who are in their thirties and forties. Fibroids are also most common among African American women.

Fibroids are usually firm, circular lumps that often occur in groups. They grow in one of two places: near the outer or inner surface of the uterus. When they grow on the outer surface they can easily be detected by having a pelvic exam. Others require ultrasound for more invasive study.

Fibroid tumors vary in size and are generally described in terms of fruits and vegetables i.e. peas, apples, grapefruit and cantaloupe. Mine were the size of several grapefruit and had begun to protrude. The doctor described my appearance as that of a woman six months pregnant.

Although symptoms are not always present, they can include abdominal pain, feelings of fullness or pressure in the lower abdomen and frequent urination. Other symptoms include heavy menstrual cycles, bleeding between cycles and increased menstrual cramps. Birth control pills, with high levels of estrogen and estrogen-replacement medication used during menopause can accelerate tumor growth.

Information adapted from the book, "Alternative Medicine: The Definitive Guide" compiled by The Burton Goldberg Group. Copyright © 1993, 1994, 1995.

Draining the Blood Supply

It took me two years to agree to have surgery after I was diagnosed with fibroid tumors in 1996. The doctor recommended surgery right away. She also recommended that I have a hysterectomy. After giving me the run down on what it would involve, she asked me what I wanted to do.

Because I was still able to move about freely and work with little complication, I didn't believe that the tumors were severe. Therefore, I elected to avoid surgery. I attended a healing convention at my church. When the minister laid hands on me, I immediately began to feel the tumors dissolve. However, they didn't go away completely.

When the convention was over, I decided to look up scriptures on healing and began making confessions concerning my healing. I also began listening to healing tapes by my pastor. I started out strong but I did not remain consistent. If I never learn anything else, I know now that consistency is the key to the breakthrough. As a result of my lack of diligence, the tumors began to enlarge.

By the second year, the complications were increasing. My feet began to swell and my blood count dropped to an all-time low. The tumors were draining my blood supply. This turning point led to my decision to have the surgery.

The doctor advised me that the blood count for women my age is generally somewhere between thirty-five and forty-five. Mine was eight! Not knowing what to do, and somewhat afraid, I spoke with my oldest sister. She had previously been diagnosed with fibroid tumors and opted to have the operation. Her testimony encouraged me.

My surgery was scheduled for the day before Thanksgiving, November 25, 1998. Because my blood count was so low, the doctor required that I have a transfusion a few days before. Again, I struggled with the idea before finally agreeing. I read *Psalm 91* and *II Timothy 1:7* to quiet my spirit and remain at peace.

Before surgery, I asked God to show me Heaven. He didn't answer. "Oh my goodness," I thought, "Why isn't He answering?" Isn't that the way it is generally? We often expect God to respond on our schedule.

While I was on the operating table, He did answer and began showing me marvelous things in a dream. He let me know in no uncertain terms that I was not ready to see Heaven. He knew that if He had granted my request, I would have been ready to leave the earth and be with Him. I must admit, the thought had crossed my mind.

In my dream, He allowed me to instead see Hell. As I entered the gates, I saw a figure of Satan on my right.

He watched me carefully. Suddenly I heard the voice of God saying, "She doesn't belong here. She has on the coat of righteousness." I recall seeing and hearing people scream and crawl around in the dark. They were searching for a way out. I turned away and that was the end of the dream.

This dream has made quite an impact in my life. Through it, God revealed to me that Hell is a real place and I should never endure what I saw those people enduring. He also told me my assignment: to preach and teach the Word of God so that those who are in darkness will know that they must accept Jesus while they are on earth.

It was somewhat of a "Jonah experience." After much persuasion, Jonah realized that God wanted to use him to touch the lives of people in Ninevah. In similar fashion, God also wants to use me to promote change in the lives of people all over the world.

The dream produced an increase in my level of compassion. I began to better understand the compassion God has for us.

An Unexpected Visitor

The day after surgery, one of the nurses came by to check my vital signs. My heartbeat was irregular and my temperature was 107. She informed me that I would be immediately rushed to intensive care.

Before calling the doctor, the nurse asked if she could pray with me. Although it was an unexpected and unusual request, I gladly consented. Her words and actions marked me for life. She said, "Heavenly Father, this is your child and Satan is trying to take her life. I plead the Blood of Jesus over her right now, in Jesus' name. Amen."

The moment she said, "The Blood of Jesus, my spirit began to fight the things that were going on in my physical body. From that day to this, my life has never been the same. *Leviticus 17:11* became a reality for me. There was no doubt in my mind that the life of the flesh really is in the blood.

I honestly believe that had it not been for that nurse's prayer and the mere mention of "the blood," things would have turned out much differently. Trust me, it was no coincidence. God orchestrated the entire ordeal.

I still wonder how the nurse knew that I was a child of God. Perhaps she had heard me pray. I never saw her again and I often wonder if she was an angel.

Ministry Begins

When I returned home, some awesome things began to take place. God was ready to perform a "good work" through me right away. I couldn't move on my own because I was very sore and extremely weak. For this reason, I had to rely on my husband and others to assist me in even the smallest of tasks.

As I rested, I listened to a tape series by Dr. Creflo Dollar. It was appropriately titled, "Anointed Because of the Blood." As I meditated on what he said, I suddenly became stronger and the presence of the Lord filled the room. In His presence, ministry began.

After the Holy Ghost ministered to me, I was able to get out of my bed without assistance. I knew that God was carrying me and by His strength I was able to walk around the room.

Astounded, my husband rushed up the stairs to see what I was doing. He couldn't believe his eyes. There I was standing …without pain or weakness. When he walked into the room, God spoke to my spirit and advised me to lay hands on him. He had been experiencing pain in his neck. When I finished praying, I removed my hand from his neck. He was healed that very moment.

We sat on the bed together in awe of the miracle God had just performed. Hearing us, one of the visitors downstairs came up to see what was going on. But the room was so charged by God's glory, she could not enter. Eventually, I motioned for her to come in. Again the spirit of the Lord commanded me to do the extraordinary. I began to prophesy over her life. As I did so, she fell to the floor under God's power.

By now the second visitor had come. It is not my practice to allow people in our bedroom, but under God's instruction I invited the second visitor in. As he and my husband listened carefully, I began to prophesy over the man's life. Not only that, I began to share things with the two of them that God was revealing in my spirit concerning other people.

Later that day, my husband phoned the people I had spoken of while prophesying. As they would each appear, I began to pray and prophesy again. This went on for nearly five hours as the Holy Spirit ministered through me. By nightfall, three of my dear friends who served on the intercessory prayer team at my church showed up. Finally, the Holy Spirit gave me the release to end. Exhausted, I fell into the arms of one of the sisters there and began to weep like a baby. I laid down and slept the rest of the night.

From that day to this, I have not experienced any of the symptoms that generally follow surgery or illness. I am totally and miraculously healed. Thank God for Jesus and the nurse who pleaded His blood over me!

FIGHTING THE GOOD FIGHT
Chapter Five

In order to win in life, you must have faith. The Bible gives an elaborate list of the faithful in Hebrews 11. The chapter begins with this familiar scripture; "Now faith is the substance of things hoped for, the evidence of things not seen. For by it the elders obtained a good report" (*Hebrews 11:1, 2*).

There was a popular song out a few years ago that said, Who's report will you believe? The answer followed, We shall believe the report of the Lord. Later in the song, the leader asks, Are you healed? Are you free? Are you filled? Do you have the victory? Each time the choir answers, Yes!

It's a great song. But how often do we really apply it to our lives? More often than not, we believe the devil's report. In other cases, we believe the world's report. Think of how you respond when the news anchor paints the picture of a grim economy. Consider how you react when the doctor delivers an alarming report concerning your health or the health of a loved one. Do you immediately run to the phone to tell someone what you just heard? Or do you take control of the situation by recalling what God has already promised you in His Word?

You see, it's one thing to say that you have faith. But it's an entirely different situation when you can actually demonstrate it. Faith is an action word. It brings the result we desire.

Thoughts and words dictate our actions. Whether positive or negative, they shape our destiny. Death and life are in the power of the tongue (*Proverbs 18:21*). We choose life when we agree with what God says. Likewise, we choose death when we agree with anything opposite to what He says.

The Old Testament records, "…I have set before you life and death, blessing and cursing: therefore choose life, that both thou and thy seed may live: That thou mayest love the Lord thy God, and that thou mayest cleave unto him: for he is thy life, and the length of thy days…" (*Deuteronomy 30:19, 20*).

The woman with the issue of blood experienced the magnitude of God's power when she spoke her healing into existence. If you study the scriptures closely you will notice that she said she would be healed before she actually received her healing. In other words, her response was based on her faith.

"For she kept saying, if I only touch his garments, I

shall be restored to health. And immediately her flow of blood was dried up at the source, and [suddenly] she felt that she was healed...And [Jesus] said to her, Daughter, your faith (your trust and confidence in Me, springing from faith in God) has restored you to health...."

Mark 5:28,29,34, AMP

What confidence! She not only believed that she could be healed, she said it out loud over and over again. And isn't that what God tells us to do? "Keep on asking and it will be given..." (*Matthew 7:7 AMP*). Faith-filled words produce positive results!

Expect to Receive

Since God never changes, you can expect Him to do for you what He did for the woman with the issue of blood. Therefore speak those things that you desire. No matter what it looks like now, don't waste time talking about it. By doing so, you give more power to the thing that currently exists. Instead, spend more time speaking those things that you desire. In other words, speak your way out of the thing you're in, into the positive thing you desire. Faith is NOW!

If you're in a financial bind and need more money, don't say, " I can't pay this bill." Instead say, "I can do all things through Christ (*Philippians 4:13*) and my Heavenly Father knows what I need even before I ask (*Matthew 6:8*). According to your Word Lord, I will ask and ask again, until I receive the finances I need to meet this obligation." Remember God can't deny His Word. It must accomplish His purpose.

Don't expect this to work if you're asking God for something that is not His will. He won't honor anything that would cause harm or confusion. You can't say, "Lord, get rid of that man's wife so that I can marry him." Or, "Destroy my enemies right now Lord Jesus! And kill my husband too, while you're at it!" It doesn't work like that. You must ask Him to do things that are according to His will.

Create Your Own Destiny

We are each created in God's likeness. When we see Him, we shouldn't be surprised. He says in His Word that when we see Him, we will be like Him. Like a father and his son, we not only have physical features like God, we have the same creative ability He has. He spoke the entire world into existence. He said, "Light be" and light appeared.

By speaking your way through each situation, you will create the destiny you desire. You don't have to be in a difficult position for this to work. Begin to make confessions your way of life. It is one of the greatest investments you'll ever make toward your future.

Look up scriptures that apply to your situation and begin to say them on a daily basis. If you need a house, look up scriptures on houses and add them to your list of confessions. If you need peace, look up scriptures on peace. The same rule applies where your healing is concerned.

Listed below are confessions to live by. God's Word is His will. By opening your mouth and speaking God's will over your life, you will produce positive results. God rewards the diligent, so get in the practice of saying them out loud every day. Soon you will begin to see things change. You'll experience favor unlike anything you've ever known before and your life will never be the same again!

1. By the stripes of Jesus I am healed and made whole (*Isaiah 53:4*; *1 Peter 2:24*). There is nothing missing or broken in my life.

2. When I call on the name of the Lord, He will hear and answer me. In this I am confident (*1 John 5:14*).

3. God will heal me whenever I am wounded or brokenhearted (*Psalm 147:3*).

4. I have no need to worry, because God will take care of me (*Matthew 6: 25-34*). Therefore, I surrender my cares to Him (*1 Peter 5:7*).

5. By the Blood of Jesus, I am justified, redeemed and made righteous. God ignores the sins of my past and will not punish me for them (*Romans 3:24, 25 AMP*; *Romans 5:9; 1 John 1:7*).

6. Because Jesus shed His blood for me, I can fulfill the will of God for my life and do good works in His name (*Hebrews 13:20, 21*).

7. I do not have to suffer tribulation

(persecution) of any kind, because God shelters me with His presence through the Blood of the Lamb (*Revelation 7:14, AMP*).

8. I will not be in bondage, neither will I fear death, because Jesus has rendered the devil powerless for my sake *(Hebrews 2:14,15)*. I will dwell in the abundance of peace that I have received through the shed blood of Christ (*1 Peter 1:2*).

9. I can do all things through Christ because He gives me the strength I need to succeed (Philippians 4:13). Therefore, I am successful in everything I do (*Psalm 1:3*).

10. I overcome all things – worry, defeat, depression, sickness, lack and poverty – by the Blood of the Lamb and the word of my testimony (*Revelation 12:11*). I am healthy and prosperous in all things, because my Heavenly Father wants only the best for me (*3 John 2*).

A NEW WAY OF LIFE
Chapter Six

If confessions are not already a way of life for you, you may want to make a covenant with God as you rededicate your life to Him. A covenant is "an agreement between two or more parties, that should never be broken." It also establishes commitment and must not be entered into lightly.

One way to solidify your covenant is through communion. Taking communion is vital to spiritual and physical health. In fact, Jesus encourages us to do it often. It symbolizes the body and blood of Jesus that was shed for you and me.

Consider making communion a part of your regimen, particularly when you begin a new task, set a new standard or need a closer walk with God. Taking communion is not something you do only at church. Communion can be taken at home, in the hospital or where ever you are at the time. It can also be taken with someone you're making a covenant with…a family member, business partner or friend.

Miraculous Testimonies Concerning the Blood

My husband, Charles and I have seen some miraculous things happen over the years as a result of the blood (communion). I recall one example, in particular, when Charles was doing mission work in South Carolina. He eventually took a job there and decided to take communion because he wanted to experience supernatural increase and promotion.

In less than three weeks he was promoted and literally began operating in the Joseph anointing! Joseph experienced God's supernatural favor everywhere he went and in all that he did.

We've also seen burdens removed and lives changed through our ministry. Here are just a few of the testimonies we've received.

Our entire church made a commitment to take communion for thirty days. As a result, everyone who needed a job or transportation received it!

My wife and I were on the verge of foreclosure. We took communion for a period of time and not only were we able to keep our house, we were also able to refinance it at a rate of 4.5%!

I am a college student and I needed tuition assistance. I took communion one night and the next day I received a check in the mail that covered the exact amount needed!

I made a commitment to improve my grades. After taking communion, I and two others were the only ones to receive an "A" out of a class of 300!

We had been experiencing difficulty in our marriage. After a while we began taking communion together. As a result, we have a better relationship with each other and our children!

I had not heard from my daughter in 4 months. I began taking communion and believed God to heal our relationship. Soon after taking communion, my daughter visited the church where I pastor and later she began visiting my home again!

My granddaughter was extremely fearful and shy. When I began taking communion and interceding on her behalf, she experienced immediate change!

After sharing the awesome testimony of my healing and deliverance from fibroid tumors, many people ask me how I achieved such victory. This list summarizes the steps that led to my healing. Each one of them has been explained in this book. Use them to renew your mind and discover a whole new way of life.

Remember, God will always do His part, but we must first commit to do our part.

1. Spend time with God daily. Read His Word and incorporate specific scriptures in your prayers.
2. Make confessions daily. After you've mastered saying them once a day, you should begin to say them

several times a day to experience dramatic results when needed. It's like exercise, the greater the intensity, the greater the results!

3. Always acknowledge that you are the righteousness of God. Say it to yourself over and over again. Your mind must be renewed to this concept so that you will be able to cast down feelings of condemnation and discouragement.

4. Remind yourself that there is life in "the blood." By taking communion and remembering all the benefits you have as a result of the shed blood of Jesus, you will begin to experience the "good life" God desires for you *(Ephesians 2:10, AMP)*.

5. Every time God does something good for you, share your testimony. It brings hope and encouragement to those who hear it.

I encourage you to read this book over and over again until the principals in it become a reality in your life. No matter what you're going through now or will go through in the future, God's desire is for your total well-being, spirit, soul and body. Make no mistake about it; there is Life in the Blood!

The Blood

An inspirational message by Apostle Juanita Ford

By the Blood of Jesus, I can wake each day,
By the Blood of Jesus, I can arise and pray.

By the Blood of Jesus, I have a study time,
By the Blood of Jesus, I find it's truly divine.

By the Blood of Jesus, I have the wisdom of God,
By the Blood of Jesus, things are not so hard.

By the Blood of Jesus, Who is the precious Lamb,
I talk to the Father, Who is the Great I Am.

By the Blood of Jesus, He is my Savior,
By the Blood of Jesus, I live in divine favor.

By the Blood of Jesus, my hands are anointed,
By the Blood of Jesus, I am appointed.

By the Blood of Jesus, the Word in my ears,
By the Blood of Jesus, I eliminate all fears.

By the Blood of Jesus, I am strong,
By the Blood of Jesus, I can do no wrong.

By the Blood of Jesus, I am the head,
By the Blood of Jesus, I am lead.

At the cross of Jesus, the devil was defeated,
Through the Blood of Jesus, God knew what I needed.

By the Blood of Jesus, I have divine health,

By the Blood of Jesus, I have abundant wealth.

By the Blood of Jesus, I lay hands on the sick,
By the Blood of Jesus, they will heal quick!

Think about His goodness and all that He has done,
By the Blood of Jesus, I have already won!

By the Blood of Jesus, I am made of dust,
By the Blood of Jesus, I rid the spirit of lust.

By the Blood of Jesus, I am a millionaire,
By the Blood of Jesus, I cast away my care.

By the Blood of Jesus, I am out of debt,
By the Blood of Jesus, all my needs are met!

TO CONTACT US

If you would like to share your personal testimony with us or let us know how this book has been a blessing to you, please contact us.

FULL BENEFITS APOSTOLIC MINISTRIES INTERNATIONAL, INC.

If you would like to know how to receive Jesus Christ as Your Lord and Savior, feel free to contact me personally:

CONTACT INFORMATION
Post Office Box 90706
Columbia, SC 29290
Juanitaford27@yahoo.com
(404) 556-0867 Mobile

ACKNOWLEDGEMENTS

If you would like to invite Jesus into your heart today and begin a personal relationship with Him, read this short prayer aloud:

Repent of Your Sin

Father God, I recognize and admit that I am a sinner. The Bible says in 1 John 1:9 that if we confess of our sins, He is faithful and just to forgive us and cleanse us from all unrighteousness. Therefore, I repent of my sin, those that I can remember and those of which I am not aware. By saying these words, I receive Your forgiveness and I am in right standing with You.

Confess the Lord Jesus Christ
(Personalize)

Your Word says in Romans 10:9-10 that if I confess with my mouth the Lord Jesus and believe in my heart that You raised Him from the dead that I shall be saved. I believe Your Word and I make a quality decision to give my life to You today. As of this moment I AM SAVED! In Jesus' Name, Amen..

Date: _____
Time: _____

Begin a New Way of Life

Congratulations on the decision you have just made. Here's what you need to do next to begin living a victorious life in Christ.

1. *Read the Bible and pray daily.*
2. *Find a church that teaches the Word of God clearly and accurately and with understanding.*
3. *Attend church services regularly and you will grow spiritually.*

Receive the Baptism of the Holy Spirit

To experience a closer walk with Christ, receive the baptism of the Holy Spirit with the evidence of speaking in tongues. Every born-again believer has the right to speak in tongues. The moment you were saved, the Holy Spirit moved into your heart. When you pray in tongues, you will experience more of God's power.

Luke 11:11-13 says that the Father will give us the Holy Spirit when ask. In other words, we will receive the gift of speaking in tongues when we ask Him with confidence. "If a son shall ask bread of any of you that is a father, will he give him a stone? or if he ask a fish, will he for a fish give him a serpent? Or if he shall ask and egg, will he offer him a scorpion? If ye then, being evil, know how to give good gifts unto your children; how much more shall your heavenly Father give the Holy Spirit to them that ask him?" Therefore, ask, and you shall receive.

ABOUT THE AUTHOR

Apostle Juanita Ford is a native of Marianna, Florida. An international teacher and conference speaker, Apostle Ford has traveled extensively to faraway lands that include Germany, Belgium and Alaska.

A graduate of Rhema Bible College in Tulsa, Oklahoma, Apostle Ford also completed the selective Minister's Education Development program offered by Dr. Creflo A. Dollar through World Changers Ministries in College Park, Georgia.

Apostle Ford is married to Apostle Charles A. Ford and together they minister the life-changing message of Jesus Christ all over the world! In the years ahead, the couple plans to extend their ministry to include a Christian bookstore, Healing and Spiritual Clinic for Women with Fibroid Tumors, residential homes for low-income families and a Christian resort. The Fords also plan to establish a series of classes throughout the United States for those who operate in five-fold ministry.

Through the Word of God and personal testimony, Apostles Charles and Juanita Ford are making a tremendous impact in the lives of people both domestically and abroad!

www.ingramcontent.com/pod-product-compliance
Lightning Source LLC
Chambersburg PA
CBHW062114290426
44110CB00023B/2808